MW00932764

INSPIRING TRUE STORIES BOOKS FOR LITTLE BLACK GIRLS

I am
Amazing

Inspiring True Stories of Courage, Self-Esteem, Self-Love, and self-Confidence

Paula Collins.

© Copyright 2022 - Paula Collins

www.paulacollins.online

paula.collins@paulacollins.online

It is not legal to reproduce, duplicate, or transmit any part of this document in either electronic means or in printed format. Recording of this publication is strictly prohibited and any storage of this document is not al owed unless with written permission from the publisher except for the use of brief quotations in a book review.

This book is a work of fiction. Any resemblance to persons, living or dead, or places, events or locations is purely coincidental.

Contents

Introduction

Hello! Do you realize how amazing you are?

You are exceptional. You are completely unique. Always remember that! You are the only you there is in the entire world, and that's out of billions of people!

The world has many big and small hurdles in store for you. Sometimes you might think that you can't make it. You might get very scared or doubt yourself. However, I want to tell you a secret. Everybody feels like this from time to time! Even adults.

In this Inspiring Stories book, you will meet other amazing girls. These girls overcome their fears, show great inner strength, and reveal their bravery.

Of course, you can show all these qualities too, but you must start believing in yourself. That is exactly what this book will help you learn to do.

You can shine your light in your corner of the world and bring that light to other people when you let go of fear and keep learning lessons. When you believe in yourself, you can accomplish anything. You are an Amazing girl.

Brielle's First Day Of School

First you're going to kindergarten, and now you're doing science projects with your classmate. Time flies when you're in school, but one thing is for sure, starting a new grade can be terrifying. It's all fun and games when you're picking out school supplies and clothes, but when you step foot onto the campus, you have no idea what to expect, or who you'll meet. That's all a part of going to school, so there's no need to be scared. Everyone is a little nervous on the first day, but you'll get the hang of it. Especially when you make new friends.

Then that's when the fun starts and the day will go by, just like that!

The alarm blares in Brielle's room. It's 6 AM and Brielle does not want to get up for school. She groans and wraps the pillow over her head, hoping it's all a bad dream. Unfortunately, her mother calls her name from the kitchen, and she's forced to get up. She turns off the alarm and stretches her arms and yawns. It's her first day of middle school and she's not looking forward to it. Yesterday, her mother took her out shopping and bought tons of new, stylish clothes for her, as well as all the latest school supplies.

The smell of bacon and eggs are calling Brielle's name, so she skips downstairs to a wonderful breakfast. Many thoughts were roaming her mind, as she sat down at the table.

What would the teachers be like? Will she make friends, or will she be a loner? The nerves began to settle in.

"Good morning, sweetheart!" Her mother smiles. Brielle shakes her head quickly, to snap herself out of the clouded thoughts, before answering,

"Morning, mom," Brielle says. She picks up the fork and digs into her breakfast, which brings a small smile to her face.

"This is delicious, as always, momma," Brielle wipes her mouth. After her meal, Brielle rushes upstairs to put on her new clothes she set out the night before. Brushed teeth and hair, she looks in the mirror, feeling confident with her outfit choice.

"Hopefully the day goes as smooth as my outfit is," Brielle thinks to herself, before grabbing her backpack and heading downstairs.

"Don't forget your schedule!" Her mother exclaims. Brielle double checks her bag and grabs her schedule. When looking at it, the nervous thoughts begin creeping in again,

Where is the G building? What If I can't find it? What if I'm late because I can't find my classes? If I get expelled I'll never be able to see my friends again!

Before she knew it, her mother pulled up to the school and Brielle's heart began to beat out of her chest with her palms becoming clammy.

"Mom, I'm really nervous, I don't know what to do," Brielle confesses.

"Brielle, you will be fine. I promise. Everyone is nervous too, don't worry," Her mother replies.

Brielle nods and hugs her mother goodbye, gets out of the car and watches her drive away.

Is it too late to call in sick?

Brielle's nerves were growing and growing within each minute. It felt as though she was in a box while everyone else was outside of it, having fun. No friends, just herself, all alone. Brielle walks around with her schedule tight in her hand, curiously looking around to find her first class. Brielle doesn't have time to keep searching, she has to ask someone for help. She walks up to a girl by the water fountain. Nervously, with her hand shaking, she taps her shoulder and asks,

"Hi, there, I don't mean to bother you, but could you help me find my class?"

The girl turns around with a big smile,

"Hi, there, sure! I'd love to help"

The girl glances at the schedule and smiles wider.

"It looks like we have the same first class, English. Do

you want to hang out?" Instantly, Brielle smiles and replies

"That's such a relief, I had no idea where I was going to go,"

A giant weight, weighing down on Brielle's shoulders, was finally lifted. One of her worries is gone and now she can focus on making a new friend. The girl introduces herself as Sarah. Sarah loves to meet new people and Brielle asked for help, she wanted to help. She, too, is nervous, but asking for help makes everything better. They talk and laugh, all morning until the bell rings. They were having so much fun together, that they forgot they were at school! Brielle and Sarah walk to their first class together. They sit and introduce themselves as the teacher calls their names.

When Mary is called, she doesn't back down and when she tells her class about herself, the class claps. That wasn't nearly as bad as she thought it would be.

Mrs. Garcia, her teacher, is really kind. She helps everyone in need and makes Brielle feel like she can accomplish any task. After some tasks and getting to know each other, the bell rings and it's time for the next class. Brielle thanks Sarah for helping her and hopes to see her at lunch. As she looks at her schedule for her next class, she builds up more confidence to ask someone for help. The school staff directs her to her next class around the corner.

"This really isn't so bad." Brielle thinks to herself.

She arrives in class on time and picks out her seat. Eyes gazing around the room, she sees classmates chatting and laughing with each other. It's a new class, which means she is a bit nervous, but she can do it. Class begins and Brielle is very attentive to her new teacher. She follows directions and is excited for the upcoming projects throughout the year and

In a blink of an eye, the bell rings and Brielle is heading to her next class. She runs into Sarah again and they walk together to their next class, because Sarah is in it too.

It's lunch time! Sarah and Brielle sit together at lunch. Sarah takes out her turkey and cheese sandwich, and Brielle takes out her peanut butter and jelly sandwich.

"Are you still nervous?" Sarah asks and takes a bite of her sandwich.

"I forgot that I was nervous! I guess I'm not anymore." Brielle smiles and takes a bite of her sandwich and when they're done eating, they play soccer together. Brielle realizes how much fun she's having and how the nervous feeling she had when she arrived was now gone. They played and played, until the bell rang. Brielle felt confident to take on the rest of the day. Even during her other classes, Brielle's confidence to take on the day really helped her. Meeting her classmates and doing classwork, really helped ease her mind of all the worries she was having.

At first, she thought she wouldn't be able to get to her classes or make friends, but she is and she can't wait for the next day, when she meets with Sarah. Brielle's mother pulls up to school and asks her how her day was.

"You were right, I had such a fun day! I was afraid of not making any friends or getting to my classes on time, but I had help from a friend and that made the rest of the day so much fun!" Brielle exclaims.

"See, I knew you could do it. Doing things for the first time can be scary, but there's always going to be help along the way," Her mother said.

Brielle's first day of school was a success, and now she can't wait to take on the second day.

After we muster up the courage to do something scary, we realize it's never as bad as we think it is. Our thoughts can play a big role in telling us whether or not to do something. Most of the time when our brain is telling us NOT to do something, doing it can be good for us. It's our brain's way of protecting us with unfamiliar things.

Stepping outside of our comfort zone is important. We can grow and learn new things if we let ourselves experience it. Good things happen when we branch out and try new things. After all, if you're feeling stuck or scared, you can always ask for help. You're never alone.

We all need help sometimes and it's okay to be nervous. It's a part of being human and it'll get easier within time. When you've done it, you've succeeded and can take on anything! Remember, there's a first time for everything, but the more you do it, the more comfortable you become. It's like riding a bike or swimming!

Don't let negative thoughts stop you from doing

what's best. You can do anything you put your mind to, as long as you believe in yourself and have the confidence and courage to do it.

Unconditional love for animals

Do you love animals? Have you ever wanted to take care of other living beings? Do you overthink what might happen in the future? This story is full of love for animals and the teaching to stop worrying so much about what might happen.

Kyla was a little girl who loved animals very much. So, for her, seeing a bunny, a dog, a bird, or any animal was a reason to feel immensely happy because she felt that they were the sweetest beings in the world.

She wanted to hug them, caress them, and talk to them.

Sometimes when she saw a dog in the street, she would ask its owner for permission, and then she would pet it. Her noble soul made all the animals come to her and let her pet them, and they would do the same, whether it was the dogs licking her, the cats rubbing on her legs, or the birds watching her from a safe distance.

One day she was at home watching a program on the children's channel, the one she liked best. But there was something around her that made her lose her concentration. It was like a repeated noise that, over and over again, made her miss scenes from her program. Although, at first, she didn't know what it was, she soon turned off the TV and concentrated.

It was raining outside. Her city always had rain all around.

But soon after she managed to hear the noise, she knew what it was about.

She got up and tried to follow the noise, which was barely audible. It was very low. But as she walked, she began to hear it more and more intensely. She reached the front door and stuck her ear to it. She could hear it on the other side.

She opened it carefully and saw her garden, where her mother had flowers, medicinal plants, and a series of beautiful plants of many colors. That's where the sound she now heard came from.

She saw some leaves move and stepped back. Her father had warned her to be careful with the snakes that could hide inside the plants, but she moved them gently and looked because she already recognized the sound.

Behind an aloe plant stood, like a little ball of fur, frightened, a small, completely wet kitten that looked at her frightened and meowed surely at its mother.

Quickly she picked up the cat and took it inside, ran to the back room, took a towel she had especially for these cases, and wrapped the little animal that, although it looked scared at first, now seemed to be grateful for the warmth and stayed still.

-Don't be afraid, kitty, I'll take care of you.

The cat saw her and meowed.

-Are you hungry? I'll get you some milk.

She went to the kitchen, and there was her mother, who at first was surprised by the animal she brought with her, but she already knew her daughter. She rescued any animal she came across.

-Another one of your patients?

-He was in the garden.

-Poor thing, let's give him some milk.

-Yes, that's what I was coming to.

The mother helped him warm it up a bit and put it on him, and the cat immediately began to lick. He was hungry.

The cat spent that day very much at ease. First, Kyla played with him, and soon the little animal felt confident with the help of a rope and a ball tied on end. They had hours of fun.

That night, when her father arrived, mom told him about the new guest, and he showed up in her room to meet him.

-Hi, daddy said Kyla.

-Hi, little one. I see you have a guest.

-Yes, he's beautiful.

She told him what had happened and how she would take care of him until he had a new home. Kyla loved all animals, but cats were her favorite. She had never had the opportunity to adopt one, only to help them while their owner appeared or while she found a home for him.

-Would you like to adopt him? -asked her father.

Kyla's eyes sparkled with joy.

-Really?

He nodded.

-Although if the owners show up, we'll have to give him up.

Kyla accepted the proposal, although, in her eyes, there was a slight shadow of sadness.

Kyla decided to name the cat Pellet because when she saw him, he looked like a little ball of fur, only wet, but now, when he slept, he turned into a fluffy ball that she caressed for hours.

But having saved Pellet, she now felt a great fear that

the cat's owners would show up, for no doubt he had not been born that long and the mother cat would be sad for him, or there would be a child missing him. This began to eat away at Kyla's mind. Although she enjoyed Pellet, she was always thinking if this would be their last day together.

Time went by, and that scared and wet kitten in the garden had now become a big cat with the look of a king who slept wherever he felt sleepy.

Kyla always loved her cat because, besides being hers, he was unique. His all-white color was only distinguished by a heart spot on his back, which, although barely visible when he was small, was now more marked. Her cat was unique.

This also caused him a bit of fear because that spot could be what was necessary for the real owner to identify him.

One thing the family liked to do was to go to a nearby mountain on Sundays. So after Pellet's arrival, he also went climbing the mountain. Kyla would put him in a special transparent backpack with holes for him to breathe, put him on her back, and they would go to the mountain, although Pellet would mostly sleep.

On one of these trips, a man kept seeing Kyla,

especially her backpack with Pellet.

He seemed hesitant, but then he became animated and walked up to her, who was with her parents, and after swallowing his breath a couple of times, he spoke:

-Hello friends, good morning -he told them.

-Good morning, neighbor. -Said the father, who lived in the area.

-I think they have my cat.

The dreaded day had arrived for Kyla. For now, she would have to return to Pellet.

-Well, said the father, we've had him for quite a while. Are you sure he's yours?

-That spot on his back is unique. One day I left the door open by accident and never found him again. I'm glad he's okay, and he looks well cared for and full of love. -Turning to Kyla, Do you love my cat very much?

Kyla nodded, thinking full of terror that the next thing that man would do would be to open the bag and take Pellet. Such was her fear that she felt her eyes burning and tears welling up.

-Don't be like that, the man hastened to say, I see you have the cat well taken care of, and I see him very peaceful. I think he is in the right place. You have had him longer than me. Now he is more yours than mine. I only ask you one thing, fill him with lots of love.

The man turned his back and left. He turned around and waved goodbye. That was the happiest day for Kyla. The anguish for the owner to appear and take the cat away was over.

She realized that for a long time, she had thought about losing Pellet, and everything turned out better than expected.

Kyla learned that giving love has good results. She had a living being that followed her around the house. When she had a cold or felt terrible, he was by her side, loyal to her, and that anxiety and fear only increased something that, in the end, turned out better.

Don't think so much about tomorrow because things will turn out differently than you fear, and you love animals very much. They are noble beings and willing to love you if you let them.

The cycle of pets

Have you ever had pets at home, and sometimes they are no longer around and remain a nice memory? This is the story of an adventure of a little girl who loves animals very much and learns the cycle of life.

Ellie had an immense love for all animals. She even liked snakes. When she went to the zoo, she regretted that the animals were locked up there, so she chose to see those giants where there was a good habitat for them or that were rescued, and it was an excellent option to have them there. She would see the snakes in the terrarium and visit the birds in the open areas with flora.

She loved going into a place filled with lots of butterflies, she would stand still, and they would start to stand on her shoulder and head. She even had a picture of a blue butterfly on the tip of her nose.

Likewise, she loved larger animals, such as dogs, cats, and even tigers. She imagined that lions had soft manes like her stuffed animals and that real bears were plush and warm like her cloth teddy bears.

On the street, when she walked, she would meet different dogs or cats that greeted her, the puppies would wag their tails and lick her, and the cats would rub her feet.

She wanted to adopt them all, but her parents did not allow it; they were not pet owners because they said dogs were naughty and would break the furniture or pee in the corners, and cats had the bad habit of sharpening their nails everywhere, birds either because they did not deserve to be imprisoned in a cage and fish did not, because they demanded a lot of maintenance in the aquarium, one less chick because they died soon and this made her sad.

It was quite a feeling for Ellie to love animals and not

be able to have one at home. She prayed that one day her parents would relent a little and allow her to adopt. She promised to take care of it and do whatever it took to make it well.

One day, on her way home from school, she found something that made her stop in her tracks and felt her heart shrivel with sadness and tenderness combined.

Behind a large piece of junk was a wet cardboard box. From inside, there was a wailing sound. She approached it, got down on her knees, and saw that sad little eyes were looking at her and pleading.

-What's wrong? -Ellie said.

The little dog cried a little louder as if trying to tell her what was wrong.

She grabbed it gently. It was a brown dog, a puppy. It must have been born a little while ago, but it was already opening its eyes. It had been abandoned. It was wet and very cold.

As she picked him up, she stroked him for warmth. He was heavier than she expected, so she opened her backpack, took out a towel she used to dry herself in gymnastics, wrapped the dog like a taco, and hugged him, stroking him with a little force to warm him up.

A few minutes later, the puppy seemed warmer and stopped crying.

Ellie knew that leaving him in that crate was not an option. Who knew what his fate would be? She didn't know what else to do but chose to pick him up and take him home. When she was close, she put him in her backpack.

-Shsst, don't go making noise, my parents don't want puppies in the house. I'll keep you in my room.

-How did it go? -Her mother greeted her when she came in.

-Well, Mommy, I'll be right back.

She ran up the stairs to her room. Her mother was surprised. She always left things in the dining room and began to tell many stories.

Once in the room, Ellie made room in the closet, placed a box, put on a blanket, and accommodated the puppy. Although, he looked at her with a grateful look, he no longer looked so sad and felt comfortable.

Her mother called her from the kitchen, and she decided to get changed and go downstairs quickly, but not before asking the puppy again not to make any noise.

She told her mom that she needed to go to the bathroom, and that's why she had come in so early. She pretended that the day was normally going, but she would run to her room every chance she got to see the puppy.

When everyone had gone to sleep in the evenings, she would take him to her bed and let him sleep curled up, careful not to let him cry for his mom.

She sneaked milk from the kitchen and spooned it to him, warm to help him feel better.

Even though he was such a little puppy, he spent a lot of time lying down, as if he was very exhausted.

Every day, before leaving for school, she would give him food and tell him the same order:

-Don't go and make noise, or you may be discovered.

The puppy watched her and said nothing but seemed to understand her.

Ellie cleaned the waste produced by the puppy and changed the cloth she had put on him so he wouldn't get an infection. Then, when no one was watching, she would throw him in the washing machine, where his mother would wash everything together, and they wouldn't notice.

On the third day, when she returned from school, she went upstairs to greet Toby. As she had already put the night before her puppy, she wanted to pet him, greet him, and hope he would walk or play. She still didn't know what she would do with him because she couldn't keep him, but one day at a time.

As soon as she opened the closet door, she saw Toby lying down with his paws stretched out. She touched him, and he didn't move, his eyes were open, but they didn't look at her. The little dog had died.

Ellie could not help it. She began to cry inconsolably, she was heartbroken, and her crying could be heard in the whole room as if she were a little girl. Her mother, who heard the noise, appeared next to her, worried about what was happening.

-What about that little dog?

-I rescued him, but he's already dead, said Ellie in tears.

It was a while before she could tell everything that had happened, crying and crying. Now she expected not only to face the loss of Bruno but also a strong scolding from her mother.

-Did you take care of Toby by yourself these days?

She nodded.

-I know you are very sad about everything that happened, but think about this, Toby was already having bad luck, wet and alone. You were the only one who listened to him and didn't hesitate to rescue him. Maybe he would have died faster, hungry and cold. You gave him a warm bed to spend his last days.

These words seemed to soothe Ellie; maybe he was sick, and she helped improve his last moments. Her mother was by her side, hugging and talking to her about how she had done a good job.

They buried Toby in the yard, and her mother told her that she had been a responsible child to take on all the burden of caring for him, but when everything was a little out of control, she should have asked for help; that's what mom and dad were there for.

Life is a cycle, those pets we love are just passing through, and at some point, they will go somewhere else. Therefore, we must love them and protect them. Also, when we are in a complex situation, we can always ask for help from our parents. They are there to help us.

Exhausted mom

Have you ever stopped to think about how hard your mom works? Do you know that she puts in a lot of effort? Our parents make many efforts and sacrifices, so everything at home runs smoothly. This story is a vivid example of that.

Zuri and Chloe were two sisters who were a year apart; they usually spent the year with half a day at school, and when they got home, a good part of the afternoon studying and preparing for the other day. Although vacation times were somewhat boring, the two shared the day at home, playing games, watching movies, and playing a console, lengthening the hours of solitude they both had to endure. There were days when there was a nanny, but they did not like it very much because she put them to do homework, wash dishes, pick up the mess and even sweep. On the other hand, when they were alone, they did not have to do anything. They just had to enjoy themselves or wait for the time to pass until mom came home from work in the afternoon.

Both sisters woke up early for a moment when their mother would come and give them each a kiss on the forehead and always told them the same thing.

-You behave well, try not to make too much of a mess, and remember, you play with one thing, put it away, and move on to something else.

They both nodded their heads and turned over to continue sleeping. Between dreams they listened to the instructions, the meals were in the refrigerator, they had to heat it, to call her by video call when they woke up, to write, not to neglect the cell phone so they could contact them when she had time.

They both answered with a nagging:

-Yes, mom.

When Zuri and Chloe got up, they walked around the house, looked for food, ate breakfast, and cleaned themselves. One of them got on the phone, and the other turned on the TV. When Zuri finished eating, she left her plate on the table, Chloe left the paper roll with a long strip on the floor and the towel to dry her hands on the floor when she left the bathroom.

The lights in the bedrooms were on. The microwave door was open, with the light reflecting off one wall.

The mother called by video call, and Zuri answered:

-Hi, daughter; where's Chloe?

-Over there.

-Call her to talk.

-Chloe!

At once, she came up and showed herself on camera, waving her hand in greeting.

-Did they eat? -asked the mother.

They both nodded.

-Did you have the lights on in the rooms?

They both looked at each other, and Chloe went to turn them off after smiling.

-Please, turn off the lights, it's to take care of the planet and my pocket too, electricity is expensive.

-Yes, mom, said Zuri.

-What is that light?

Zuri moved the camera in the direction shown by her mother, and it was the microwave.

-Close that microwave door immediately.

Zuri got up and closed it.

-They just got up, and already the house is upside down; please, be tidier. I'm tired of so much work, daughters, help me. I barely have enough strength to prepare things for the next day.

-Okay, said Chloe, who was already in front of the camera again.

Mom gave them other indications and said she would

call them again after lunch. She had to work.

Zuri suggested to Chloe that they play in the room; they went in, opened the toy closet, and took out everything, a giant cloth bag full of many things, from baby maracas to stuffed animals that they hadn't seen for a long time. They made a river of stuff on the floor and entertained themselves for about 15 minutes.

Then Zuri suggested they watch a kitten app she had downloaded the night before, and there they were given lunchtime.

That's how they went through the day. In every room they went through, they left a mess; they played ghosts with the blankets on the beds and then left around the sheets and pillows, everything, the bare mattress in the room.

That afternoon when Mom returned, as soon as she walked through the door, she found a house that looked like it had been hit by a hurricane, everything upside down, the living room furniture cushions on the floor, the dishes from the day's meal accumulating flies, the refrigerator half open with the light coming through the crack, the bedrooms with everything on the floor, the bathroom with the lid up and a mess of products.

-Girls! -was the mother's way of showing how upset she was.

They both appeared to greet her with joy, but the smile they were wearing disappeared when they saw the mother's face.

-What did I tell you earlier?

They both remained silent, searching for the answer.

-To have order in the house! Look how you have everything, now besides doing everything I have to do, I will also have to tidy up this house because you were incapable.

The mother made a strange grimace and went to her room.

Both sisters looked at each other with guilty faces and walked almost noiselessly, peeking into the room.

Mom was sitting on the edge of the mattress, on the bed, with her hands. She was holding her head, frustrated. She looked terrible like she was trying to deal with a lot of things.

Zuri motioned for her sister to follow her, and they both went into the living room.

-I think we messed up, Zuri said.

-Yes, we made a bit of a mess.

-We have to do something, let's tidy up now, and when mom comes out, she can see things in order and be happy, okay?

The other nodded, and they immediately started tidying up.

Soon after, they had washed the dishes, tidied up the bathroom, and picked up every single toy in the room, it wasn't perfect, but at least they had evened it out a bit. The beds were poorly laid out, but it was just a matter of mom smoothing it out, and it was ready.

When mom came out, already resigned to the fact that she would have to get down to work to tidy everything up, she was surprised to see that the house was tidier.

She saw the girls looking guilty and waiting for her reaction. The mother knelt to be at their level and told them to come closer, to hug them.

The three of them gave each other a long hug, and then she gently pulled them aside to speak to them.

-I understand that you want to play, and that's fine; I like you to have fun, but it doesn't cost you anything to tidy up a little. How long did it take you to organize what you did just now? Nothing, just a little while; I spend all day at work, it takes me an hour to go, an hour to come back, I prepare your lunch for tomorrow, mine, I tidy up things at home when I go to do the shopping, it takes more hours, I wish it wasn't like that, but it's hopeless, it's what we have to do. Thank you for helping me to tidy up.

The three of them hugged each other, and from that day on, they began to play with things and tidy them up. In the evenings, when mom came home, instead of each one staying in her own space, they would help her with something or at least keep her company, tell her things, and even complain about each other, just like any other family.

Our parents go out of their way to get things done. Zuri and Chloe learned this from seeing their mom exhausted from picking up messes.

It's okay to play like any other child, but for every mess you make, pick it up and support your parents; they go out of their way to ensure you are comfortable and don't miss anything.

Respecting the rules

Have you ever gone to other houses and been given rules that you don't understand why they exist? Do you feel like breaking the rule you are being asked to follow? This story is about how a little girl understood that an uncle was right to ask her not to do something.

Mia's relationship with her uncle was strange because she saw him from time to time. He had excellent humor, they played, and he always told some very funny joke that made her laugh. He also had a side of the character. He said that he liked people to do things correctly to comply with the rules because that was how the world could function correctly.

She was also a big fan of animals, especially dogs. She liked cats, but not so much.

One of the reasons why she liked to go to her uncle's place was because he had a dog named Olaf, a very playful German shepherd with whom she got along very well. They played, they chased each other, and he licked her until, in the end, she felt that all her skin smelled like dog, but she did not mind because she loved him very much.

Although her uncle was severe with the orders to the dog, they could only play in certain areas of the house, he could not take her to others, and they had time for play. He said:

-Dogs that are left too long on soft things like playing turn into kittens, and I want a dog to take care of.

The uncle worked as a mechanic, and in the evenings, he would leave the dog inside the garage, next to the house, guarding it in case someone wanted to get in, the German shepherd would bark at him, and he wouldn't dare.

The uncle had the idea that if Olaf played too much, one night, instead of protecting the workshop, he would open it so that whoever wanted to enter would be able to get in comfortably and look for what he wanted to take.

The trips to his uncle's place happened from time to time. They lived in the same city but from one end to the other. Mia's mother, her uncle's sister, was the one who took her every two weeks or once a month to visit and stay for a day.

-Niece! -said the uncle with joy, let's see which fish wears a tie.

-I don't know, said Mia after thinking about it for a while and giving up.

-The neck!

Everyone laughed because he always had a bad joke to tell.

That day of the visit, besides having Olaf in the back of the house, there was in the living room, on one of the furniture, an orange cat, asleep with its paws stretched out and deep.

-This one is as he wants to be, - said Mia's mother to

her daughter.

-What a comfort this cat is, lazy, - said Mia.

-It's Luciano, - said the uncle -he's been here for a few days.

-He's cute. Can I play with Olaf? -said Mia.

-Yes, but on one condition.

-Okay.

-You can't bring him in the house for anything.

-But this is where we always play.

-This time, it can't be because these two don't get along. They play in the workshop.

After the siblings ate, Mia's mother left and said she would be back in a few hours and that she would stay with her uncle. She asked her to behave well and to comply with the rules.

Mia resigned and went to the workshop. There was a big and badly parked truck, leaving a small space to play. When Olaf felt her friend nearby, she looked for play, and they chased each other several times around the truck.

Mia hit the bumper three times, and in some parts, she had to pass sideways because of the wall or the tool machine.

-My uncle didn't know how to park this, she said, it's ugly to play like that.

Mia looked inside the house, but her uncle was not around. She saw Olaf and snapped her fingers to be followed. The dog did not move. What he did was tilt his head with a questioning expression.

Mia looked at him again and said:

-Come, I permit you.

The dog, still hesitating, followed her, sniffing everything, feeling that he was not on his ground. When they reached the living room, the place where they usually played on previous trips, the dog stopped and put on an expression of anger.

Luciano, the cat, stood up, and all his hair stood on end.

Instantly the dog went after the cat, and the cat went after him in a fit. The two began to chase each other, taking whatever they could find with them.

Ornaments fell to the floor, a small library with books fell, a car door was on one side, and it turned and hit the floor, and in less than a minute, the whole house was upside down.

Mia chased the dog, trying to stop it and also the cat but had no luck.

-What's going on here? -said the guy who appeared screaming. He took three steps and grabbed Olaf by the leash, dragging him while he shouted furiously at the cat, who was watching him angrily from afar.

The uncle left the dog in the workshop and locked him up. Now his cold gaze fell on Mia.

-Remember I asked you not to let the dog in?

Mia nodded ruefully.

-What was going to happen?

-They were going to fight with the cat.

-That's right, you see what happened.

The uncle turned his back on her and went to the

backyard, then came back with a broom, a mop, a bucket, and disinfectants.

-Do you see how wet the floor is?

-Yes.

-The cat or the dog peed while fighting. You're going to clean it up and pick it up.

What took the dog and cat less than a minute to destroy took Mia two hours to pick up, tidy up, mop the floor, and clean thoroughly, she was sorry that her uncle was upset.

When she finished, the house was sparkling clean and didn't seem to have had room for a dog and cat fight.

The fear Mia had was that when her mother arrived, the uncle would accuse her, but she didn't. Maybe the lesson of having to clean the whole floor and tidy every corner without anyone's help had been enough.

She learned that she should not break the rules in someone else's house and that she had to be attentive to what her elders told her. If she was in someone else's house and they gave her an order not to touch or move the pet, even if it bothered her because she could not play well, she had to obey it because there was a reason for it.

The next time she went to her uncle's house, there were no cars, and she was able to play with Olaf all over the workshop, but she had to make sure she met the cat.

Sometimes there are rules that we don't like, but we are in someone else's house, or an adult asks us to do it, and we must respect it. They have their reason for asking you not to do something. If you want to do it, ask permission first.

The stretching playdough

Have you ever wanted something so badly that you felt like deceiving to get it? Do you think it's right to lie to get what you want?

This is the story of a girl who believed she didn't have enough playdough and did whatever it took to get more.

Janelle was very excited because she would finally start school, and they would ask for a list of supplies. She laughed when she saw her parents putting their hands on their heads when they saw the supply list - they were asking for many things. It was a great moment for her because she would have so much. Among the things they were asking for in the school supplies, there was some play dough that she had to bring. Since there were several children in the house, 4 more besides Janelle, there were many supplies to buy. Janelle bought a box of 8 playdoughs of different colors.

This is what Janelle loved the most. When she had it in her hands, she started looking at it, softly putting her fingers in it and dreaming of opening it and stretching it, and making many shapes. She felt happy with that blue box, with those long playdoughs. She was proud of them, and when she got to school and took them out with the other supplies, she saw that almost everyone in her class had 60-piece playdough sets, many colors and bars, and Janelle's was only 8.

"This isn't fair; how come I have this pitiful box of 8 playdoughs, and my friends have 60 pieces? I'm so embarrassed to bring the poorest box of all", Janelle thought when she saw her friends with all that playdough. She thought her parents didn't love her, that they bought her the cheapest thing they saw at the store, and that's why she was now going through this embarrassment.

So, when she got home, she made her parents see what she was thinking and asked them to explain why they had bought her so few playdoughs.

They told her that's what the list said, and it was what was appropriate. Also, she should multiply it, there were 5 boxes of play dough, and her friends probably had few siblings.

But Janelle came up with a plan. The next day, she said that her playdough was lost, that it wasn't in her bag, and that maybe a child had stolen it.

Her parents didn't say much, but they went and bought her another box of play dough, and although it wasn't the 60-piece one, she now had 16 playdoughs. So, it was double what she had the day before.

Proudly, she prepared a special box and began placing all the playdough inside. There, she left her 16 pieces, which looked wider, less embarrassing than pitiful 8. 16 was better than 8, there was no doubt about that, but after a while, she thought that 16 playdoughs were still very few. She had to have more with her.

Again, that night she told her parents that on her way home, her backpack opened, and the playdough box fell into a sewer, and no matter how hard she tried, she couldn't retrieve it.

Her parents had told her there was no luck with these playdough sets and that she would have to figure out how to take better care of them. But then they went ahead and bought her another identical box.

When Janelle came out of the bathroom, she saw another box of eight identical playdough pieces on her study desk. So now she had 24 playdough sticks, three of each color. This filled her with joy, and she spent some time arranging them in different ways to her liking. But she realized that 24 was still not the 60 she desired, and she thought she would have to keep figuring out how to get that amount.

So, she decided that the next day, she would change her plan so there would be no suspicion. She told her parents that her teacher had demanded that they have a box of 64 playdough pieces, not just one with eight and that she had purchased the wrong school supplies. As soon as she said this in the dining room, Janelle saw that her father was upset with her from the way he looked at her.

"It's curious how you keep losing that playdough", he said. "It's been happening to you all these days, but I don't think it's happening to any of your other classmates, right?"

"Well, that's what I think. I already told you that they got lost on the first day, and on the second day, I accidentally dropped them down the sewer. Things happen", she replied.

"A strange coincidence", her father said.

"Yes, it is", Janelle agreed.

Her father pondered everything he had heard for a moment.

"I don't know why all of this is happening. It's strange. I've been thinking about it. I think I will go to school with you tomorrow to talk to this teacher and help me understand everything, especially about the first box you lost. It's not right for someone to take away your things, especially at the start of the school year. It's a big effort to gather every school supply for a child who lacks education".

Janelle felt her stomach churn, and everything went dark because if her dad did that, her lies would be exposed. She couldn't allow it. Everyone would know, even her friends, her grandparents, everyone. She would be the family thief, the cheater who invents lies. All the teachers would look at her with suspicion, and it would be the label for her entire student career. The playdough thief, they would call her. So how was she going to prevent this from happening?

"Without a doubt", Janelle's father continued, "if the playdough is lost instead of stolen, and you go and find them, even the one that you dropped down the sewer, then I don't think I'll have to spend hours looking for problems with this teacher and asking for permission at work to deal with this minor problem".

After this, there was a tense silence, and Janelle thought for a moment before speaking almost in a whisper.

"I think I'll look for them at school tomorrow; maybe they're on my desk in the classroom".

"I hope so", her father said.

The next day, as if by some miraculous occurrence, all the playdough reappeared, even the one that had fallen down the sewer. When they asked Janelle, she said that maybe it didn't fall and that it was just her imagination.

"Yes, I found them". Said Janelle.

Her father acted as if he were amazed.

"It's wonderful that you found all of them".

After this, he gave her a big hug and a kiss on the forehead.

Janelle knew that her father knew the whole story. Perhaps he had found the playdough in her bag and didn't say anything and left her with this lesson so she would learn what honesty meant. Her father had given her a way out.

Perhaps, if she had lied again after this, he wouldn't

have given her a way out, but from that moment on, she knew that she had done wrong. She never made that mistake again.

Honesty is essential. You should never try to deceive others, especially not your parents, who make a great effort to provide you with everything you need.

Amusement Park

Can you imagine being next to your parents one moment and then losing them the next? What would you do at that moment? This is the story of a girl who experienced it firsthand, one of the most terrifying moments of her life.

Anna was extremely excited when she found out that an amusement park had arrived in her city. It had everything: roller coasters, shooting games, bumper cars, a Ferris wheel, jumping castles, and everything a respectable amusement park should have, including the biggest cotton candy she had ever seen.

The family planned to go to the amusement park in the following days since it was something unprecedented in the city. It would be an incredible weekend, and they would have a wonderful and exciting day. It was an emotion born from her belly that rose and filled her with great joy. Anna imagined herself eating the biggest cotton candy, asking for the pink and blue ones, drinking soda, sitting in the front seat of the roller coaster, and screaming until she was hoarse.

Among the fun things they saw on the day they finally arrived at the amusement park was the inaugural show, a series of fireworks that formed a series of figures in the sky. Combined, blue, red, and yellow balls exploded, forming those lights that seemed like stars had descended. Everyone was mesmerized by the fireworks. Although Anna, while watching them, felt a great urge to go to the bathroom, she didn't want to miss a second of the show.

At that moment, while watching the show, she heard her cousin Michael telling his mom that he had to go to the bathroom, that she should take him or something like that, she thought she heard.

"Mom, I want to go to the bathroom", said Michael.

"Okay, but you can't go alone. You have to go with your cousin Harry".

"Okay, fine, we'll go together. We'll be back soon, so we don't miss anything".

"Okay, but don't separate, please, and be careful not to go with anyone. Both of you are protected. That way, neither of you will get lost".

Realizing that her cousins were going to the bathroom, Anna saw the perfect opportunity since she wasn't the only one who needed to go. So, she looked in the direction of her mother, who was entranced with the show. She preferred not to disturb her and quickly headed towards the bathroom, wanting to return as quickly as possible. As she was walking, she passed through a crowd focused on what was happening. She passed a series of people and began to lose sight of the others. She started to panic as she looked at the people, and none of them were her family. Many crazy thoughts passed through Anna's mind: "Will I never see my mom, cousins, or dad again?"

Anna started walking with more dedication, looking at people in the park, searching for a reference point, but everything seemed the same to her. She didn't know where she was anymore, and she couldn't even find the bathroom, which was why he had walked away. She didn't see her cousins either, only unfamiliar faces. She stopped trying to find her cousins and tried to retrace her steps, trying to remember where she had come from, but she got more and more confused as she looked around. Everything looked so similar! When she felt like it had been an eternity, she couldn't hold back her tears and started crying with fear, imagining all sorts of things, thinking that she would now live in one of those houses full of parentless children.

She tried to control herself, not wanting to cry, but she was worried and overwhelmed. She cried and tried to speak, but not a single word came out of his throat. "Mom, the mommy, come for me, please, mommy!" she cried and screamed, but it was so noisy that no one heard her, not even herself. She felt like she was making those sounds, her face drenched in tears.

She screamed louder, and everyone around her was so focused on their things that they didn't realize a little girl was there, helpless and lost. Once again, she faced all those thoughts that hit her and the terror she felt. What was going through her head was horrible, and she started running as fast as she could without paying attention to the direction. There were people she didn't know everywhere. She was going crazy. A small little girl, now without parents, had suddenly been left alone forever. That's what he thought.

"How could I walk away from Mom and my family without telling them? I made a big mistake by doing that. I'm sorry, mommy, I'm sorry; I shouldn't have done it", Anna said to herself. With her face wet with tears, she kept running, pulling at people's clothes as she could and shouting, "Mommy, where are you, mommy?" She hoped one of those people would be her parents looking for her. When she saw them, she would hug them and be between their arms, but every face she encountered was unfamiliar.

Finally, a lady with very white hair and a sweet look saw her crying inconsolably and terrified and asked her in a very nice voice, "Did you get lost, honey?"

Anna nodded, still crying.

The lady didn't say anything else but gently took Anna's hand and walked with her while she looked at people in the crowd and asked her where she had seen her parents last and if she remembered the exact spot. When Anna started feeling safe because she was being helped by an adult, she calmed down and thought more rationally. She remembered they had been leaning against a wooden bar that was characteristic of the area and let the lady know.

The lady led her through the path that Anna had indicated, and they were already close to the woods when she approached a man and asked, "Is this your daughter?" The man shook his head. She continued to move forward, asking here and there, looking for her parents.

Anna was searching for a familiar face when she finally spotted one that she recognized right away. She felt like the happiest person in the world. "Mom!" she shouted joyfully while pointing to the lady so she could take her to her. When the lady put her down on the ground, she ran towards her mother and hugged her with great happiness.

Now Anna didn't want to let go of her mom. She was scared that she would lose her again and never wanted to be alone again. While she cried with joy, fear, and all the emotions she had felt, her mom also cried. After calming down, they thanked the lady and said that she had done a great deed.

Anna stuck to her mother like glue for the rest of the night. She didn't want to be separated from her. She even forgot to go to the bathroom. Later, her mother explained that it was good that the lady helped her, but she should never wander off alone and be careful with whom she goes. This time, she was lucky to find someone with a kind heart. Still, if she ever got lost again, the best thing to do was to look for a police officer or someone in authority who could help her find her parents.

Never, ever wander off from your parents without their permission and without them supervising where you are.

The New Teacher

Have you ever experienced a teacher change in the middle of the year? How did it make you feel? Did it hurt? This is the story of a wonderful teacher who has to leave and another who arrives and how this impacts a little girl.

Johanna was excited when she saw her friend Annie enter the classroom with a folder full of many cutouts that she knew he had promised her. It was the plan they had to be able to finish a bulletin board they would use in an exhibition.

"The teacher, Emma, said we would finish this today", said Johanna.

Annie looked away.

"She told me you would do the coloring part, and I hope you do because you're really good at it. Will you do it?"

"Of course I will. I want to do it. I've been waiting for days," replied Johanna.

Annie had not worked much besides what he brought in the folder. The bulletin board was mostly Johanna's work, who had taken care of drafting what would go on it and its distribution. When Annie saw the bulletin board, he started talking to it as if it were a living thing.

"You probably didn't want the teacher, Emma, to leave, right?" he said to Johanna.

Johanna watched him from a distance and said nothing.

"At least we're here to complete it; this person who arrives will help us improve it. I'm sure she'll love it, so don't worry. Johanna and I will take care of it".

The next day, the new Teacher stood in front of the

children and asked them to put their notebooks under the desk and pay attention. Then, they were going to play a game of spelling words, each one more difficult than the last, and the one who remained standing at the end would win. Whoever made a mistake was out.

All the children were spelling, and several started to drop out as the game became more complicated. But they were doing well, and it seemed like the game would go on for a while.

Annie, who was a little hurt by the new Teacher, said, "I'm not going to spell anything".

After saying this, he put his backpack aside, crossed his arms over his chest, and had a surly expression. When it was his turn again, the Teacher insisted that he try, but he deliberately made a mistake, so he was out of the game. Johanna seemed to want to emulate what her friend did, and when it was her turn, with a surly expression on her face, she also deliberately made a mistake and looked challengingly at the Teacher.

On that day, after the game ended, when Johanna was engrossed in a book, the Teacher sat next to her and smiled.

"Teacher Emma told me that you love creating

things and that you were preparing a beautiful poster", she said.

"Yes, that's what I used to do, but life changes, right?" Johanna replied.

"I love building things, and so does my husband. It's our passion. I like to paint, and my husband carves wood; we make great things. If you want, I can bring you some drawings to put on your poster and a piece of wood to put in the corner. It would look beautiful", the Teacher offered.

"I don't want to make any poster. It seems silly to me, and I don't want to waste my time on it. I don't want anything from this school, and I don't want you either", Johanna said, becoming angry. It seemed like everything she had been holding inside had burst out.

The Teacher stepped back and said nothing more, giving her space. Then, during recess, Johanna threw a ball with force at Raquel. "What a great day to catch! Who wants to play that?" the Teacher suddenly appeared out of nowhere and said.

"Not in a million years do I want to play that. I don't want to play anything. The recess is ruined now, too", Johanna replied.

Later, when the class resumed, the Teacher asked everyone, "Would anyone like to email Teacher Emma? It would surely make her very happy".

Everyone seemed pleased and gave their approval. "Well, it's easy. Each of you will write the message on a sheet of paper, and at the end of the day, we'll send it to her", the Teacher explained.

"I won't send anything. I don't like that idea", Johanna said.

The Teacher seemed to realize that Johanna was hurt, and she was not the only one; Annie had also shown it, but it was more palpable in Johanna. She probably had many questions for Teacher Emma. In fact, Johanna was thinking about many things, like "Why did she have to go back to that city? How could she leave us alone?" She was too sad to say it, but she felt bad. She was even angry about showing it to others.

The next day, when Johanna entered the classroom, the Teacher had a large envelope in her hand. "We have correspondence from Teacher Emma", she said. Johanna shrugged and went to her seat. The Teacher opened the envelope and showed pictures of Teacher Emma, where she was, and even some cows she had posed with. Inside was a note that the Teacher began to read aloud.

Johanna, although she looked the other way, could see everything out of the corner of her eye and was very attentive while listening to the Teacher.

"My dear children, I miss you more than you can imagine. I know the new Teacher is fortunate to have you and will fill you with love and education for the rest of the year. I really like what I'm doing now, commitments I couldn't avoid. I think about you all the time, every day. Johanna, please finish that beautiful poster you were making; it will be worth having it adorning the classroom all year long".

Sincerely, Teacher Emma.

Johanna didn't say anything but felt her eyes watering and burning. During recess, she was alone that day, thinking a lot about what had happened. She walked through the park, sat on the benches, kicked some stones, and remained silent for a long time.

"I thought Teacher Emma would be my teacher all year", she told her new Teacher. Finally, Johanna accepted the pain that was eating away at her.

After a while, the Teacher said, "People come and go from our lives. When that happens, new beginnings can be difficult and painful. But Teacher Emma will never forget you, and I know you won't forget her either".

Johanna wiped away a tear with her thumb.

When the children settled in their seats, the Teacher took Johanna's hand and showed her a box full of beautiful drawings and pieces of wood made by a true artist. There was even a bottle with a design inside. The poster would be incredible.

Johanna looked surprised, took a deep breath, and began to feel better. She started to go through the box and saw that there were many things she could use. She looked at Annie and asked her to come over and try new things. The girl looked at her new Teacher and said, "Teacher Miel, I'm lucky to have you; you're very good. I've had two good teachers this year, Teacher Emma who I won't forget, and you, who I'll never forget and who showed me the love of teaching with this".

Changes happen everywhere; people come and go, but never forget the importance they have.

The Popular Video Game

Have you ever wanted a game but haven't been given it even though all your friends have it? Do you know the value of imagination when you let it run wild? This is the story of a girl who discovers how she can have endless fun.

Bella had been asking her mother for a while to please get her a game that everyone in her school had. It was one of those portable consoles with options to download new games every month. All her friends talked about it. For her, it would be the best thing ever because any respectable gathering of friends involved sharing opinions and playing with one of these devices, which, if connected to the TV, allowed you to play with others.

"All my friends have one of those consoles. Even the boys already have it. So it's not fair that I don't have mine," said Bella.

"That's not the right way to talk to me. Think about how you treat me," replied her mother.

Bella looked at her and felt frustrated. She knew she wouldn't be lucky that time.

"According to a study, children who use these video games can have better concentration and less attention deficit, which would help me in school," said Bella, trying to negotiate.

"Putting together puzzles has the same effects, plus others. Putting together pieces has always been good for the brain. Go get the castle puzzle you asked for and never put together. Go put together the Legos you have in your room," said the mother.

Bella thought her mother's response was just to get her to put together that Lego or that puzzle. Every time she asked for something, it was the same response. She thought putting together those things was for fools, a boring game, spending hours looking for the piece at the tip of the window in hundreds of identical pieces or that Lego that fell apart over time. That was for babies.

"No one wants to come to a house where there's no video game to entertain themselves; update yourself, mom," said Bella.

"There are many other options. For example, you can put on a movie with popcorn and have a great time. I assure you," replied her mother.

Bella had been insisting for a while, and she knew her mother was starting to get upset. She was very patient, but there was a breaking point where she said no more. The girl knew that many friends had that video game, although not everyone did. Some didn't have the money to buy it, but her mother earned well, so she could give it to her if she wanted. But her house was different because there, she was allowed to watch television, but only educational programs about animals in the jungle, kids teaching about science, values, morality, and others.

Many of them were fun, but Bella wanted something else, and that video game could give her that.

"We'll invite friends for dinner," her mother said. When Bella found out which family they would invite, she thought it would be boring because there were two girls; Sofia and Chloe, and she wouldn't have much fun with them. "I want you to be kind to the girls and play while the adults share," her mother said.

On the day of the meeting, Sofia started talking to Bella and asked her what games she had to entertain herself. Chloe was also interested in knowing what they had to pass the night. Bella didn't know where to turn because she knew they weren't referring to puzzles or Legos but to a console or something "more fun." "My mom bought me a game with a mustached doll that crushes other animals and has to rescue someone in a house. I don't remember the name right now," said Sofia. "I got one with princesses that we dress and decorate," said Chloe. Bella knew they were talking about consoles. Bella didn't want to delve into that; she didn't want to be embarrassed, so she took her to the room to look for something to play with. They took out some boxes with toys that she hadn't played with in a long time, and Chloe saw Bella and said, "Where's the game room?" asked Sofia. "In the closed room over there, but we're redecorating, so we can't go there now. There's a mess, dirt, dust, and paint smell." "Well, where else?" "The attic, but there's not much there." "Let's see." The three girls set off that way. They unfolded the roof ladder and went up one by one. Upon arrival, they saw a pile of dusty boxes and old dishes that nobody used. There was a lot to explore and snoop around.

"Mom has all this stuff accumulated here."

"Why?" said Chloe.

"No idea. She says they're memories and valuable things." Bella didn't understand her mother's love for things from centuries ago. Old junk that could go well in the trash. But she didn't want to comment on anything bad; she had promised to behave well. Sofia took a square box piece and threw it to the other side of the attic to kill boredom. "There must be many of these boxes here," she said. "I think so. I don't know," said Bella. Sofia turned a box over and emptied its contents, and when she did, she found something that interested her. She looked at the other two with joy.

"I think we can make a castle for ourselves and live there like queens," said Sofia.

"I would be the queen," said Bella, "since I live here."

"Well, you can be the queen, but we can be queens, too," said Chloe.

"Three queens?" said Sofia.

"Why not?" said Chloe.

They spent a good while creating a castle to everyone's liking, like building with Legos, but using the boxes accumulated in the attic. The plan was that they were the queens and owners of that castle, a game that they changed later when someone tried to invade, but they defeated them with cannonballs, throwing small boxes and things.

Soon, dragons appeared that knocked down the castle, and kings tried to take possession of it.

Time got away from them. They realized it was time to go when Sofia and Chloe's parents called them from downstairs. They said goodbye, took their coats and promised to see each other soon. The adults seemed to have had a good time too. They said goodbye with plans to see each other again soon.

"Mom," Chloe said to her mother, "we left a castle there. I want to go back and keep playing."

"When you want, you can come back; we will arrange for us to come again."

After they left, Bella saw that her mother was looking at her.

"A castle?" she asked.

The mother said nothing but went to the attic to see what mess they had made. Bella thought they were surely going to get scolded for the mess.

"A castle?" the mother asked again.

She went up and looked around and saw the mess, boxes everywhere, disorder, a bigger mess than before.

"I see you didn't get bored," she said.

"No, we didn't get bored; we had a good time."

"I'm glad you had fun instead of thinking about that game."

Bella thought she could invite other friends to that castle, as she was passionate about it. Not always the trendiest game is the most fun, there will always be toys of the moment, but they are not as fun as imagination when you let it fly.

The neighbor needs help

Have you seen that there are people who need help? Have you discovered how much you can do for someone with a little effort on your part?

The best way to help someone else is to surprise them by being kind, so you show them you care and make a difference. That's what this story is all about.

Marie was working on a puzzle of a beautiful macaw, she was looking through all the multicolored feathered pieces to find the one that went in that space, she was a little frustrated but at the same time she was enjoying putting the sections together.

She heard something outside and looked out the window. It was Mrs. Emily who was on her way home, someone too old to walk with great effort with a cane, she had something on her leg and this made it difficult for her to walk, later she would know that it was a splint, apparently, she had had an accident.

He put down the puzzle and decided to go find out what was going on.

-Dad

-Tell me, daughter.

-Mrs. Emily walks with a cane and has something on her leg.

-That's too bad. Let's go see her, maybe she needs our help.

Marie liked the idea of going to see what was wrong with the lady. She liked how her father liked to help others and was kind. She shook his hand and they walked outside in the direction of the lady's house.

They knocked on the door and the lady opened it a couple of minutes later.

-Hello, John. -She said, - How can I help you?

-My daughter saw you arrive just now. We came to see how you were doing.

-Oh, how nice of you. Please come in.

The woman sat down. Her leg was hurting.

-What happened to her? -Marie asked.

-I was going out to buy fruit for the week and I slipped on the corner, my foot bent. It didn't break, but they put this on it so it will heal, I have a crack. Thank goodness it didn't break because at this age the bones don't weld the same.

Marie didn't think it was lucky at all, she thought it was a bad thing. She agreed that at least the lady hadn't had a broken bone.

-That's too bad.

-Not so bad, in a few weeks you'll see me bouncing and happy. I'll be good again.

-How are you going to do your things? -His father asked.

-I think I'll ask the boy on the corner to come and help me, the errand boy. I'll have to pay him, but no way.

They visited her for a while longer and then went home. That night while they were all at the dinner table, Marie talked about Mrs. Emily and asked about her family, if she didn't have anyone to come and take care of her, children or siblings. Her father told her that she was single, never married and now alone in the world.

-I wish I could help her, Marie said.

-What a good heart you have, said her father.

The subject remained there, but late at night, while she was with her father solving the macaw puzzle, Marie said to him as she placed a piece, I know how we can help the girl.

-I know how we can help Mrs. Emily. We can do some things to her house so that she doesn't go from one place to another.

-How would you do it?

-Surely the doctor asked her not to walk so much, so we can help her with house chores so she can rest and be calm.

-I like the idea.

They both spent a long time thinking about what they could do to help the lady, going to check things at home, she cleaning and they agreed that they would bring her food, the mom said that now she would make the meals for one more plate and so they would bring her every meal.

-Today when we were there, I realized that there were several things to do. - Said the father.

-I saw the house a little dirty, I could sweep and mop.

-Yes, there must be something to do and we can help.

Marie's father felt very proud of his daughter for what he had proposed, he realized that he had inherited her good heart. They agreed that the next day he would propose to Mrs. Emily the help they were going to offer her.

Before closing the bedroom door to go to sleep, he said to her:

-I feel very proud of you, of that desire to help others, I congratulate you daughter.

Marie felt good and went to sleep with a very gratifying feeling in her chest.

The next day, they went and proposed to Mrs. Emily to help and after she said no, because she felt sorry to bother them, she agreed, recognizing that she could use a hand. The father began to check the house, changed some light bulbs, fixed some wires that were about to short out, in the bathroom he fixed some dripping faucets, checked a clogged pipe and fixed a humidity that had a white stain on a wall.

Marie cleaned the house thoroughly, dusted the dust, fed and pampered a Siamese cat she had, combed it and removed all the dead hairs.

He cleaned the gutters that had a lot of leaves and were causing internal leakage when it rained.

Mrs. Emily apparently felt at ease with the presence, because she went to take a nap, and father and daughter laughed when the lady snored and seemed to be at ease. Since they were both free, they decided to play hide and seek for a while. They had a lot of fun.

After checking everything inside, including eating at Mrs. Emily's table, when Marie's mother brought the food, they went out to check the plants in the yard, to prune the lawn a little and to cut some branches of an old tree that threatened to crush the roof of the house.

Marie would never forget the look on Mrs. Emily's face when she woke up and saw her house, with all the repairs done and outside clean, with the lawn flush and the plants cared for, she was impressed how young, strong hands had accomplished so much. Marie and her dad were tired from the day's work but happy.

-Thank you, it's been a long time since I've seen my house as beautiful as it is today. Everything is beautiful, thank you, thank you.

-It's an honor, we want it to get better soon, said Marie.

-Thank you for your help, princess.

The lady wiped her tears. She was moved, and she felt loved and supported.

Marie could not stand it and hugged her neighbor and gave her a kiss on the cheek.

-We just wanted to help you feel better.

-I feel much better, even my leg hurts less. Thank you.

The next few days the support was visits, some small chores, and lunch every hour.

Then Mrs. Emily said that she could cook for herself and that she had improved a lot.

For about a week, they didn't hear from her. One day there was a knock at the door. Marie opened the door and saw Mrs. Emily without crutches, and she looked younger than before, refreshed. She had something in her hands. It was a chocolate cake.

-Thank you! -Marie said to her.

-Thank you for the help. You have given me these days. More than feeling sick, I felt sad and lonely because I had to do everything by myself.

Mrs. Emily looked very happy and grateful, with a deep affection and thankfulness that came from the bottom of her heart. The three of them ate cake and tasted coffee and tea.

No matter how old you are or what you do, a simple gesture can brighten someone else's life. You can't imagine the needs that others have. Don't be afraid to help.

Every idea you have put into action, just like Marie proposed to help the neighbor and made her convalescence more bearable, you can mark help with others. You have a special gift in this world, and only you can share it. It is time. Be kind, and help others feel amazing and you will feel amazing yourself.

Made in the USA
Las Vegas, NV
28 November 2023

81568318R10046